1000
REASONS
YOU'RE THE
PERFECT DAD

M000216294

1000
REASONS
YOU'RE THE
PERFECT DAD

Rebecca Hall

MQP

Contents

Introduction 6

1 Love: Past and Present 11

2 Our Contrasting Styles 67

3 Playing and Laughing 115

4 Everything You've Taught Me 163

5 Our Friendship 227

6 Living Together 275

7 The Root of My Security 339

8 Your Inspiration 403

Introduction

In the twenty-first century, the role of fathers is less clearly defined than it used to be, say, fifty years ago. Back then, the stereotype was that men went out to work to provide for their families, left the nurturing of children to their wives, and got together with "the guys" every now and then to watch or play sports. Now there are no fixed rules. Men can be full-time single fathers or every-second-weekend fathers; they can be the parent who stays at home with young children or the extraordinary step-dad; and they are often the chief confidant, cook, and comforter in the household.

Of course, there have been men in every generation who realized the life-enhancing, eye-opening, benefits of having a close relationship with their offspring, but these days, as the media increasingly portrays this kind of dad, more and more men are discovering fatherhood's joys.

The perfect father isn't a saint. He is a human being with needs of his own. He can be short-tempered, stressed, and occasionally thoughtless, but his children grow up from babyhood to adulthood secure in the knowledge that he loves them so fiercely that nothing could ever shake or alter that bond. It is an unselfish, pure love that can be relied on no matter what, and it teaches them that they are lovable people who are entitled to be loved in the world.

As well as loving them unconditionally, the perfect father befriends his children, shares their interests, and frequently gets down on the floor to play with them. Long before they start school, he makes sure that they know that they are funny, entertaining, likeable little creatures. A good father gives his children the ability to approach the world with confidence, expecting to be liked by everyone they meet.

Newborn babies are like miniature computers without any software. Everything needs to be programmed in, month by month and year by year, so that they learn how to survive and thrive. Few of life's lessons can be instilled using a textbook or a CD-ROM, so the perfect father has to explain, discuss, cajole, and persuade, to set an example that his tiny descendants will be eager to emulate. There's an old adage that children will copy what their parents do, not what they're told to do, so perfect dads should do their best to show their kids how to be good citizens of the world.

Fathers across the planet and throughout the centuries have certain things in common, despite their cultural and religious differences. We all share the biological instinct to protect and the human desire to make our children happy. The very best fathers go further than this, aiming to inspire their kids to be the most fulfilled, exceptional people they can possibly be.

The feedback we give them along the way is reward in itself, but this collection aims to let perfect fathers everywhere know that their achievements have not gone unrecognized.

Why not tell your dad all the reasons why he's perfect today? You can go back to taking him for granted again straight afterward!

1

Love: Past
and Present

You've understood from the start that a child is not a possession, but a gift.

Of all the fathers in all the world, I'm so glad I got you.

You've got a huge personality, and a great big heart to match it.

Since I grew up and started seeing you as a person in your own right as well as my dad, my love for you has become much deeper.

There's a boyish quality about you I find enormously moving.

I know that there's nothing I could do that would make you stop loving me.

Even my little successes make you very proud and happy.

I'm so glad you were there when I took my first steps in life.

I always feel my spirits lift when I know I'm coming home.

You never believed that affection was unmanly.

Even when I was a baby, you had an inner radar system that told you just what I wanted and what would make me happy.

You always clapped the loudest at my school plays and cheered the loudest at my sports games.

You taught me to demand high standards from people who say they love me.

The pride on your face when I brought home my report card, no matter what it contained, made me proud of myself and determined to do my best.

You relished every moment of my childhood.

You remember exactly where all my baby pictures were taken.

You can quote my **first words**, describe my favorite **childhood** toys, and name the bedtime **stories** I liked the best.

The milestones of my childhood seem to be imprinted on your memory.

When I think back, I can only remember good times.

You always like to tell others about my achievements.

You worked so hard to give us the best things in life, and tried so hard never to let us see how tired you were.

I like to look through old photo albums and imagine you as a boy.

You still love me, even when I'm being awful.

You're a jack-of-all-trades and master of quite a few.

"My heart belongs to daddy."

COLE PORTER

You always made me feel that you were so thankful to have me.

You helped me see the strength and comfort that could come from a loving family.

You really enjoy being a father.

I like to look at your capable hands and remember all the things they do for me.

I love the lived-in quality of your face.

I still remember the feeling of my small hand in yours, and how important it made me feel.

You drop everything the minute you know that I need you.

I feel so lucky to have you on my side, rooting for me.

I always felt that you'd move heaven and earth to protect your family.

You always made me feel like a precious gift that you were lucky to have.

You took real pleasure in even the smallest of my achievements.

I'm so grateful that I got the best father anyone could have.

I treasure all my photographs that show the two of us together.

"He caught the first accents that fell from thy tongue, And joined in thy innocent glee."

MARGARET COURTNEY

Everything you gave to me is part of me forever.

You can always tell by my voice when I need cheering up.

You never spoiled me with too many possessions, but gave me all the love I needed.

You may have made some mistakes as a parent, but you never made the same one twice.

You could always make me laugh through my tears.

I like counting our genetic similarities—there's no doubt we're related.

I'm curious about everything that happened in your life before I came along.

I hope I can pass on to my kids even a fraction of what you've given to me.

I find myself becoming more like you as the years go by.

You always had a handkerchief ready to mop up my tears.

As a father, you are the epitome of unselfishness.

You always had enough time and energy for all the family, so that no one felt anything other than loved by you.

One of my greatest debts will always be to you, because you never made me feel as though I owed you anything.

You never fail to show wonder at the fact that you created me.

"All the feeling which my father could not put into words was in his hand— any dog, child, or horse would recognize the kindness of it."
FREYA STARK

You taught me the meaning of the words "unconditional love."

You made me realize that being a parent is about love and understanding, not control or expecting the impossible.

We've always shared a special connection—our own private sphere.

Love to you has always meant time spent with the people you care about.

Your main source of inspiration and motivation was always your family.

You never cared if we were the best, only that we were the best we could be.

You never minded getting your good clothes dirty when a grubby kiss was offered.

I have a photo of you holding me as a baby that demonstrates how much I meant to you right from the start.

"It doesn't matter who my father was; it matters who I remember he was."
ANNE SEXTON

You showed me continual affection, even when I pretended to resist.

Some of the things I value most about you are your little, nameless acts of kindness.

If anyone failed to see my potential, you didn't hesitate to point it out.

F.A.T.H.E.R.S.

Faithful

Always there

Trustworthy

Honoring

Ever loving

Righteous

Supportive

I have so many unforgettable memories of our crazy, funny times together.

I know I can take you for granted.

You made me feel liked as well as loved.

I'll never be too old for one of your bear hugs.

I get a pang when you cut yourself shaving.

A pat on the head from you can always make me feel cherished.

I love contrasting the strength you display when dealing with the outside world and the marshmallow tenderness you show your family.

No one else cares about me the way you do.

All you want is for me to be happy.

"To her the name of father was another name for love."
FANNY FERN

You never missed an opportunity to say you were proud of me.

Your praise means more to me than anyone else's.

You took pleasure in my first love, and then my next, never believing that your special place in my heart had been usurped.

You know me back to front and inside out.

You made me feel safe being the person I am when I am with the people I love.

You were never afraid to let me see how deeply you felt.

There are some special things you've said to me that I'll treasure in my heart forever.

You give the word "family" real meaning.

"When Charles first saw our child Mary, he said all the proper things for a new father. He looked upon the poor little red thing and blurted, 'She's more beautiful than the Brooklyn Bridge.'"

HELEN HAYES

You loved me enough to keep tabs on me, even when I wanted complete freedom.

You knew that love involved discipline, even when I firmly disagreed.

I know how to make your face light up.

There's a certain way you look at me—half smile, half serious—that's just brimming with love.

I like it that you choose to be with me whenever you have some time to spare.

Your constant little shows of affection have always led me to believe that I am lovable.

Your love taught me the importance of relationships.

"It is not flesh and blood, but heart which makes us fathers and sons."

JOHANN FRIEDRICH VON SCHILLER

You actually worried that you weren't a good enough dad, when you were head and shoulders above anyone else I knew.

The fact that you missed me so much when you were away made me feel incredibly loved.

Your need for me was never overwhelming, but always reassuring.

You have an uncanny knack of making everyone around you feel as though they are the favorite.

You never just assumed I would love you, but worked to make sure I did.

You believed in a better world, and fought to make it a place in which you would want your child to live.

"The most important thing a father can do for his children is to love their mother."

HENRY WARD BEECHER

You understood the importance of fatherhood as a life-bestowing gift.

You enjoyed the challenges and adjustments of fatherhood, and took delight in how they changed you as a man.

Fatherhood brings out the best in you.

You can remember every detail and all the emotion of the first time you held me in your arms.

Your love for me was never secret—you are proud to demonstrate it to the world.

You told me that having a child changed the whole universe for you, and that nothing was ever the same again.

You may not have been famous or set world records, but to me you are a hero.

When I first **realized** that you were a **man**, not a god, and that you had weaknesses too, **I loved you** even more.

"My father would pick me up and hold me high in the air. He dominated my life as long as he lived, and was the love of my life for many years after he died."

ELEANOR ROOSEVELT

You admired me with your heart and loved me with your mind.

You taught me that true wealth is being surrounded by people you love.

You governed gently—
something I will always respect.

You were an ordinary man, turned by love into the greatest adventurer.

You gave me wings to soar into my own space and life, but I always knew where home was.

You will always be the one great love of my life, and no one else can ever really measure up to you.

"It's only when you grow up, and step back from him . . . that you can measure his greatness and fully appreciate it."

MARGARET TRUMAN

You believe that your life has been immeasurably enhanced by having children.

You thought I was the fairest child ever to have been held in a father's arms.

I love you right down to the very last detail—the set of your eyebrows, the look of concentration on your face, the shape of your ears, and the scent of you.

Secretly, you believe that I'm better than everyone else in the world—and I think the same about you.

2

Our Contrasting Styles

You let me go my own way even when it wasn't what you wanted for me.

I love the way you treasure those awful photos from my childhood that show me with goofy haircuts and dreadful clothes.

"When I was a boy of fourteen,
my father was so ignorant
I could hardly stand to have
the old man around. But
when I got to be twenty-one,
I was astonished at how
much he had learned in
seven years."

MARK TWAIN

Let's just say that tact is not your middle name.

Sometimes I can't believe what you let me wear!

You always listened, even when you disagreed.

You understand that I have my own thoughts and opinions, and you never try to second-guess them.

You didn't expect me to be like you, but I think you are pleased that, in many ways, I am.

Your estimation of my talents
could never be called unbiased.

*Your idea of fashion was
having two shoes that
matched, but you never
minded my preoccupation
with the way I look.*

You took all my crazes seriously, even when they only lasted a week.

You didn't make me feel that there was an image of perfection I had to live up to.

You knew when to make a fuss and when to let it go.

I never felt that there was a huge distance between us.

You never minded when my socks didn't match, or when my T-shirt didn't go with my pants. You let me develop my own style.

You **remember** all the little things that are **important** to me, and you **manage** to keep up to date with my **interests**.

"My father was a statesman; I'm a political woman. My father was a saint. I'm not."

INDIRA GANDHI

My taste in music was never yours, but you always gave it a chance.

You understood when I thought you were ignorant, and never reminded me of that fact when I realized how much you really knew.

You always believed I was a credit to you—even when I clearly wasn't.

You knew my moods, and you understood when to leave me alone.

You never wanted to turn me into a mirror image of you.

I sometimes see a wistful expression on your face and realize that you fear losing me.

I regret every fight we had when I was a teen, but I know that you valued my spirit.

You let me make my bedroom my own space.

There were *certain areas* that regularly became a *battleground*, but you stayed *calm* and tried to *explain* to me why they *mattered*.

You must have felt betrayed by me on many occasions as I grew up, but you never let me see it.

You understood that when I screamed, "I hate you!" at the height of an argument, it was just part and parcel of being a silly kid.

"For thousands of years, father and son have stretched wistful hands across the canyon of time, each eager to help the other to his side."

ALAN VALENTINE

Your stories about when you were a little boy made me realize how much we are alike.

I guess I was pretty annoying at times, but you didn't let on.

You never treated my achievements as your own, but made it clear that they were mine, and due to my efforts alone.

When I **seek** your **approval**, it's because I **value** your opinion.

I ask your advice first, before I turn to anyone else.

You understood when I didn't want to talk, and you let your silence comfort me.

You're one of the wisest people I know.

"It is a wise father that knows his own child."

WILLIAM SHAKESPEARE

Every gift you ever gave me was thoughtfully chosen, even if you sometimes got it wrong.

You never made any distinction between a father's job and that of a mother.

You always pretended that the gifts I gave you were more treasured than anything else.

You never made me feel guilty for wanting to be myself.

You taught me to take pride in my appearance.

"It is **admirable** for a **man** to take his **son** fishing, but there is a **special** place in heaven for the **father** who takes his **daughter** shopping."

JOHN SINOR

You've always accepted me as I am, but you've also always known my potential.

You never made me feel I had to conform to a stereotype.

You may not be easy to please—but it's always worth the effort.

There's nothing cool about you; you're the antithesis of cool.

You always knew what I needed when I didn't know myself.

You didn't laugh at my stupid mistakes—or shout at me for them.

You showed me that there are right times and wrong times to be obstinate.

You're always tickled to see that I'm good at something you're not.

Your hidden talents still surprise me.

You didn't let me get away
with being a know-it-all.

"*Any man can be a
father. It takes someone
special to be a dad.*"
ANONYMOUS

You never made me feel responsible for you, and you never placed any unreasonable demands on my time.

My grumpiness was always in stark contrast to your happy optimism, but you always let me be myself.

The differences between us never frightened you.

When we argue, you make sure it doesn't get nasty.

I didn't feel the urge to rebel against the things you stood for.

"It's clear that most American children suffer too much mother and too little father."

GLORIA STEINEM

You always celebrated our differences, even when they made you crazy.

You sometimes took the opportunity to pass on a little sartorial advice— most of which I remember and laugh at today.

We didn't always see **eye-to-eye** on the importance of **schoolwork**, but you tried to give me **dreams** and the **motivation** to work toward them.

You didn't try to make me grow up too fast.

You had an uncanny knack of judging when I was too sick to go to school and when I was faking.

You can be conveniently deaf at times.

No matter how angry you got, you always made sure I knew you loved me.

I still have the books you gave me, even the ones I never read.

Your willingness to play devil's advocate taught me to assess my own thoughts and beliefs.

When I lost my sense of direction, you were always there to show me another way.

My teenage troubles didn't drive a rift between us, and I've always been grateful for that.

Your attempts to understand me as a teenager made me laugh, but I'm so proud that you cared enough to try.

You overlooked most of my adolescent rebellions but you stayed alert so that I didn't get into real trouble.

You didn't try to stop me from growing up, although sometimes I think new signs of my maturity made you nostalgic.

"A father is a man who expects his children to be as good as he meant to be."

CAROL COATS

You celebrated my growth and increasing independence, even though it must have been difficult to let go.

Playing and Laughing

Some of your jokes make me groan, but they're the ones that stick longest in memory.

Your boyish enthusiasm for our games made them much more fun.

Sometimes I think you're completely crazy—and then I'm glad you are.

One of my favorite things to do in the world is make you laugh.

When I hear a good joke, I can't wait to tell you.

I love the blackest, wickedest side of your sense of humor.

In some ways, you're just an overgrown schoolboy.

Our mock wrestling matches taught me self-control, and they were a lot of fun.

You were always happy to let me use you as a climbing frame.

I remember your concern when I struggled to learn how to ride a bike, and your enormous pride when I finally succeeded.

When I was a toddler, busy exploring the world on my own two legs, you understood that your lap was required for refueling.

You were rarely too busy for a game.

You showed me that there's a time and a place for practical jokes.

You made me laugh at my mistakes and learn not to take myself too seriously.

"Fatherhood is pretending the present you love most is soap-on-a-rope."

BILL COSBY

Your laughter can drive all the discontent from my heart.

I like all the pet names you have for me, even if I pretend that I don't.

I'm so glad that we share a sense of humor.

You never minded the mess I made with my toys—you often made just as much of a mess yourself.

You were good at making rainy days fun and memorable.

You dislike humor that's mean-spirited.

You used to pretend I could run faster than you.

You had a sixth sense that told you when my shrieks were from fear and when they were from delight.

You never laughed at me when it would have hurt my pride.

You always managed to see the funny side of life.

Sometimes you pretended not to notice when I was being ridiculous.

Your silly songs still make me chuckle.

Our quarrels usually ended in laughter.

Sometimes our eyes meet over the kitchen table and we burst into spontaneous laughter that no outsider could ever understand.

It makes me giggle when we're abroad and you decide to practice your foreign-language skills.

Sometimes you could tickle me out of a bad mood.

When I was being lazy you would try to inspire me with enthusiasm.

I especially valued the toys you made for me.

You never let on that Santa Claus didn't exist, even when I was far too old to believe in him any more.

I knew that those mysterious Valentine's Day cards that appeared in the mail for me were from you.

You never miss an opportunity to tell a corny joke.

You taught me that laughter can often be the best medicine.

You made me appreciate the joy of shared mirth.

When you pushed me on the swings, I felt like I was on the top of the world.

You never begrudged me a toy I really wanted.

You always made room for me to crawl onto your knee.

You took over the building blocks and created the best towers, but you made me believe that you couldn't have done the job without me.

Sometimes I got the impression that you loved kicking a ball around even more than I did.

You let me win our games until you realized that I could beat you without any help.

Most of our stock family jokes originated with you.

Your wholehearted laughter made me believe that my silly jokes were funny and that I was a true comedian.

"Every thing in this world, said my father, is big with jest, and has wit in it, and instruction too, if we can but find it out."

LAURENCE STERNE

You never made me feel
that I'd lost face.

I wish I'd never been mean
to you—but I know that you
don't hold a grudge.

*I love to hear funny stories
about the mischief you made
when you were young.*

You taught me games from your childhood that none of my friends had even heard of, and I felt special sharing your past.

Sometimes you embarrassed me—but I was never ashamed of you.

You let me "help" you with chores like gardening and washing the car when I was far too young to be anything but a hindrance.

I love the sound of your laughter.

If anyone listened to one of our wackier conversations, they might think we were crazy!

You worry that I might be bored, and you always find something fun for us to do when we are together.

I can usually make you laugh when you're grumpy.

You give spectacularly wild piggyback rides.

You're usually up for a water fight.

You always gave me what
I needed, even when I didn't
know what it was.

*You could make me laugh
until I was nearly sick.*

You showed me the fascinating things I could find in our own backyard.

When we were playing together, I knew I had your full attention.

Even if I came last in the race, I came in to a hero's welcome.

You find it enormously hard to discipline me (thank goodness).

You take such enormous delight in jokes and laughter.

I love the way you laugh at pomposity.

When I tried to express myself seriously, you didn't laugh.

You made sure that, when it was important, I understood the difference between real and make-believe.

We have some very strange and totally meaningless rituals.

"Dads are stone skimmers, mud wallowers, water wallopers, ceiling swoopers, shoulder gallopers, upsy-downsy, over-and-through, round-and-about whooshers."
HELEN THOMSON

I've always known I can tell you anything.

You can see the funny side of most things.

You made me believe that watching cartoons was as important as taking any business call.

You understood that being there is the first step to being a good dad.

You are unfailingly amused by your own jokes, even when no one else is.

You made my world a magical place.

You always had an idea that could entertain me.

You understood that kids need secret hiding places.

You were always happy to provide a quiet interlude when I was weary.

You knew that there were times when there was no place for grown-ups in a game.

You didn't mind when I jumped in puddles and splashed my clothes—or yours.

You did your best to see things from my point of view.

Forget Clark Kent—to me you were the real Superman.

You showed an interest in everything that interested me, no matter how mundane it might have seemed to you.

You always admired the nature specimens I found—like a dead leaf or a dandelion.

You lifted me high in the air and gave me a new perspective on the world.

You allowed me to show you a world you said you'd half forgotten.

You encouraged mischief, as long as it wasn't cruel.

You made the rules but were often willing to bend them.

You were never too old to get down on your hands and knees and play.

You were good at sensing whether I was in the mood for rough-and-tumble play or gentler games.

"My father used to play with my brother and me in the yard. Mother would come out and say, 'You're tearing up the grass.' 'We're not raising grass,' my dad would reply, 'we're raising boys.'"

HARMON KILLEBREW

I love remembering the games we used to play on long journeys.

You pointed out rainbows and birds'-nests, spider webs, and ladybugs.

Your practical jokes were sometimes corny, but always kindhearted.

You made sure I had plenty of time to play.

You're kind to animals; in fact, I've caught you talking to some.

You taught me how to laugh at myself.

You were the source of all the best games, and you knew all the rules.

You never minded doing something just for the sake of doing it, or going somewhere just to see it.

You're a master in the art of mischief making.

You have a vast repertoire of funny faces and silly voices.

You don't tease me in a way that hurts my feelings.

Holidays were always fun and memorable, thanks to you.

You can be extraordinarily weird sometimes—but weird is good!

You made me feel a sense of accomplishment, even when I may not have earned it.

You never let other kids' teasing
become cruel.

*We always laughed at each
other with affection.*

**You can do a very
funny imitation of me.**

"My dad always used to tell me that if they challenge you to an after-school fight, tell them you won't wait—you can kick their [butt] right now."

CAMERON DIAZ

You made games so much fun that I usually didn't even realize that I was learning new skills as we played.

You were never too tired or bored for play.

Your sense of humor is infectious, and I've certainly caught it.

Your euphemisms for bodily functions crack me up.

If there's any fun going on, you want to be part of it.

Everything You've Taught Me

"One father is more than a hundred schoolmasters."

SEVENTEENTH-CENTURY ENGLISH PROVERB

You always take the time to teach me, even when I don't want to learn.

You taught me to look and listen, to think and question.

You always explained why.

You can tell when I don't want advice, and you usually manage to bite your tongue.

You were never too proud to look something up, to be sure you were giving me the right information.

You were strict when you needed to be but I always knew you were fair.

I knew that you had rules because you loved me and wanted me to be safe.

You taught me that good manners open doors in life.

You've always been prepared to try something new, even if the results were sometimes hilarious.

"To show a child what has once delighted you, to find the child's delight added to your own so that there is now a double delight seen in the glow of trust and affection, this is happiness."

J. B. PRIESTLEY

You taught me the importance of staying rational when dealing with strong emotions.

You showed me that there's a difference between pleasing others and groveling.

You always showed me that if I thought things through, the answer would come to me.

You've helped me to treasure the simple things in life.

I didn't always make the grade in the outside world, but I always made yours.

You taught me that it didn't matter if I won or lost, as long as I tried my best.

You knew that indulging me wasn't always the kindest thing to do.

"I talk and talk and talk, and I haven't taught people in fifty years what my father taught by example in one week."

MARIO CUOMO

The best lessons were the ones you didn't even know you were teaching me.

Your trust in me made me trust in myself.

When you refused me something, I knew it had to be for a good reason.

You made sure that our home was full of stimulating books and pictures to help me learn.

You were almost always right—much to my frustration.

You showed me that it's fine to be nostalgic, but only in small doses.

**You taught me to value
the lessons of the past.**

**You always took the time to
explain things properly.**

You showed me how stories can
bring the world alive.

*You taught me that
cruelty is never right.*

From you, I learned a strong sense of fairness.

"By the time a man realizes that maybe his father was right, he usually has a son who thinks he's wrong."
CHARLES WADSWORTH

You helped me see that too much conformity is deadening.

You taught me the power that words can have, and how to use them wisely.

I could never go wrong by copying your example.

You taught me to accept others for what they are.

You showed me how to reserve judgment until I knew all the facts.

You've never let yourself indulge in knee-jerk reactions.

I learned from you that it is worth looking at both sides of an argument.

You taught me that sometimes it's right to let the other person win.

"My father always told me, 'Find a job you love and you'll never have to work a day in your life.'"

JIM FOX

You helped me let go of the idea that I always had to be right.

You made me see that there is more than one form of success.

You taught me that being a well-rounded person makes life more enjoyable.

You've shown me that hard work is important and worthwhile.

You made sure that I wasn't afraid to speak up for myself.

You showed me early on that it's always best to talk about things that bother me.

You didn't forbid things for no reason at all.

You tried to make sure
I understood the difference
between right and wrong.

*When I made mistakes, you talked
them through with me.*

You taught me to count my
blessings when I'm feeling low.

The things you taught me equipped me to go out into the world as a confident adult.

You made sure I was **independent** enough to cope on my own **when** I needed to.

Your high expectations of me made me expect the most from myself.

You taught me not to be dogmatic.

You made me see that winning is good, but just doing my best is more important.

"One moment's obedience to natural law and an ordinary man finds himself called upon to be wise, kindly, patient, loving, a dispenser of justice, an arbiter of truth, a consultant pediatrician, an expert in education, a financial wizard, a mender of toys, a source of all knowledge, a master of skills."

PETER GRAY

You taught me to accept defeat with grace.

I always felt guided by your principles.

If I had a question, you always seemed to have an answer.

You never told me the kinds of lies that other children heard from their parents.

The best fun I ever had was embarking on discovery with you.

Every day with you brought a new lesson.

You taught me not to be afraid
of being alone.

You made me treasure the
ability to be independent.

*I love the way your
interests opened up new
worlds to me.*

You haven't been afraid to learn from,
as well as teach me.

You showed me that it's not weak to admit you don't know something.

Even though you were proud of me, you never let me get conceited.

You've always insisted I should be kind and considerate to everyone, and to expect the same in return.

You made sure I was excited by new opportunities.

"He who is taught to live upon little owes more to his father's wisdom than he who has a great deal left him does to his father's care."

WILLIAM PENN

You taught me to value common sense and my own instincts.

You taught me to treasure the gifts I've been given.

You taught me to have sympathy for those less fortunate than me.

When I ask you a question, you answer it as honestly as you can.

Because of you, I respect everyone, young or old, rich or poor.

I learned from you that fear is one of the most destructive things of all.

You helped me value health,
and strive for it.

"My father taught me that the only way you can make good at anything is to practice, and then practice some more."

PETE ROSE

You've taught me to value the lessons of childhood.

You showed me that tears are nothing to be ashamed of.

You taught me to judge people by what's inside them.

You taught me that the best movies don't necessarily have to be in color.

You made me realize that I need to take risks sometimes.

You made sure I never lorded it over others when I won.

You didn't coddle me, and I'm grateful for that.

You taught me that falls and scrapes are part of life.

How many times did you tell me that life isn't fair? You were right!

You made me realize that if bad times come, good times will as well.

You always said that genius was genetic, and that I was a chip off the old block.

"Fathers, like mothers, are not born. Men grow into fathers, and fathering is a very important stage in their development."

DAVID GOTTESMAN

You made sure I had respect for the natural world.

You helped me to recognize my talents and make the most of them.

You didn't let me waste my opportunities.

Your lack of snobbishness taught me to approach others as equals.

I learned from you that a little dose of eccentricity never hurt anyone.

You never rebuked me when I changed my mind about something important.

You never let me laugh at the difficulties of others.

"Words have an awesome impact. The impressions made by my father's voice can set in motion an entire trend of life."
GORDON MACDONALD

You made sure I knew the value of money and how to look after my finances.

You taught me what it means to be a good person in the world.

You're one of the few truly altruistic people I've ever met.

You tried to avoid peering over my shoulder to correct mistakes.

You showed me that material success is hollow if it comes at the expense of love.

You made sure I understood how rewarding a career can be, but not at the expense of everything else.

You taught me to keep knocking on closed doors if I really want something.

You showed me that sometimes it's best to retire gracefully.

"From the reputation and remembrance of my father, [I learned] modesty and a manly character."
MARCUS AURELIUS

Your rules were consistent and only occasionally contradictory.

I don't ever remember you saying, "Because I said so."

You showed me that I should never simply assume that I'm right.

You made me realize how wrong it is to waste time.

You never lost your patience when I couldn't grasp what you were teaching me.

You tried to make sure you only passed on the good lessons you'd learned in life.

I'll never forget our little chats—they taught me what parenting is all about.

When you said no, you always meant it.

You taught me that the people who treated me badly weren't worth my time.

You made sure I wasn't afraid to stand up and be counted.

You gave me a sound moral foundation—and then let me make up my own mind about issues.

You've taught me to value quiet moments of peace.

Because of you, I'm cautious, but not cowardly.

Because of you, I find it really hard to waste anything!

You taught me not to be stuck in my ways.

"He taught me all I needed to know about faith and hard work by the simple eloquence of his example."
MARIO CUOMO

When I was swaggering and showing off, you brought me down to earth gently.

You said that when I get to my lowest point, that's when things will improve.

You showed me that the best way to feel better about myself is to do something for someone else.

I learned from you that there is more than one right way to do things.

You liked to teach me new skills and applaud me when I had mastered them.

You showed me that violence is usually a sign of weakness and ignorance.

You wanted me to be well educated for my benefit, not because it reflected well on you.

You never told me how to live; you just lived, and let me watch how you did it.

You are my walking encyclopedia.

You made sure I knew that bullies are the lowest kind of people.

When you caught me in a lie, I couldn't bear the disappointment on your face.

You made me value our cultural heritage.

"The best and wisest man I ever knew, who taught me many lessons and showed me many things as we went together along the country by-ways."
SARAH ORNE JEWETT

You showed me I'm not helpless—that there's always a way to get things done.

You made me realize that it's never too late to say, "I'm sorry," or "I love you."

You taught me that there is a difference between taking a risk and being reckless.

You taught me that I can achieve whatever I want in life if I work hard enough.

You've always taught me that honesty is best in the long run.

You taught me to make the most of every minute.

You taught me that only boring people are bored.

You always showed me that I have to give in order to receive.

You showed me how to care for animals and things that need my protection.

You've always asked me to think about what I can give back.

"Everything I ever learned as a small boy came from my father. And I never found anything he ever told me to be wrong or worthless."
PHILIP DUNNE

You encouraged me to develop my spiritual side.

You made me see that extremism in anything is never healthy.

Your respect for me taught me to respect others.

Your tolerance made me see good in others.

You taught me to walk, and you guided my first steps.

You were good at recognizing the moment that I learned to do something myself.

You taught me to hold out for real love in life.

When you offer advice, it never sounds like an order.

"A man's children and his garden both reflect the amount of weeding done during the growing season."
ANONYMOUS

You rewarded good intentions.

You taught me to take what life throws at me with good grace.

You embrace and welcome other cultures.

I'll always remember the way you didn't like to miss anything.

You never abused your power as a parent.

I was afraid of your anger, but only because I hated to disappoint you.

You taught me never to say,
"I can't," unless I'd tried.

"By looking at us, listening to us, hearing us, respecting our opinions, affirming our value, giving us a sense of dignity, he was unquestionably our most influential teacher."

LEO BUSCAGLIA

You made me respect the truth.

You showed me that a little bit of insecurity isn't so bad.

You didn't let me get too puffed up with my own importance.

You were never afraid to admit when you were wrong, so I learned not to mind when I was, too.

5

Our Friendship

When I was a child, you were my father; now that I'm grown up, you are my friend as well.

You've always been interested in what I have to say.

You know instinctively when I need a compliment.

I'm still astonished when you take my word for something.

It makes me proud when people tell me how much they like you.

Even when we argued, we knew we were still pals.

"Only a father doesn't begrudge his son's talent."

JOHANN WOLFGANG GOETHE

Our friendship has outlasted all change.

When my friends have problems, you always ask if you can help.

You remember things I tell you about people you've never met.

I learned that friendship is for keeps, because you taught by example.

You've always spoken to me as an equal.

I save up things to tell you that I know you'll be interested in.

You initiate discussions and ask me for my view.

You tell me the truth, even when I don't want to hear it.

When I needed to talk, you listened.

You made me realize that friendships need constant nurturing.

You taught me that true friendship is seeing the good in people and overlooking the little problems.

You always understood what I left unspoken.

You never tried to force an issue.

I've learned from you to take everyone on their own merits.

You are fiercely loyal to me.

"A shaky child on a bicycle for the first time needs both support and freedom."
SLOAN WILSON

Your generosity to my friends makes me proud to bring them home.

You remember all the little things that make me tick.

You showed me that looking from the heart is the only way to view a friend.

You remember my friends' names and why they are my friends.

When I've been at my lowest, you've always been there.

You never believed that children should be seen and not heard.

You weren't always patient, but you always tried to be.

"It is much easier to become a father than to be one."

KENT NERBURN

You taught me to be a loyal friend, because you were always so loyal to me.

You never made me look small in front of my friends.

You made me understand that friendship between parent and child is not only possible, but magical.

You never trampled on
my confidence.

You made me understand that
parents can be playmates and
soul mates, too.

*You've taken an interest in
everything in my life, from
the smallest detail to the
biggest event.*

We have never needed words to share our thoughts.

You never needed or wanted to be a stereotypical dad; you let your emotions define your actions.

You didn't mock me when I wanted to act grown-up.

You parented by instinct rather than by reading a rule book.

Your approval is always worth striving for.

Through your example, I realized that the only way to have a friend is to be one.

You closed your eyes to my shortcomings and let me find them myself.

With you I can be sincere, without worrying about saying or doing the wrong thing.

You've shown me that family and friends are the best companions.

You offer hospitality to everyone, and you've taught me to do the same.

You understood how fiercely a child wants to be respected.

I always knew that you would do the honorable thing.

You never liked gossip or malicious chat.

You've always been passionately interested in what's happening in my life.

There was always time to sit down, talk, and laugh.

You never pushed me to be anything other than I am.

You were always the first to call and congratulate me on my successes.

You let me come to you with problems in my own time.

You've always kept my secrets.

You always offer a warm welcome to guests, no matter what.

When I call home, my spirits lift when you answer the phone.

You go out of your way to help strangers in distress.

When it's raining you bring the car right to the front door.

Wherever you are, you always take the time to make sure that I'm OK.

You thought it was better to be taken advantage of than to be too cynical about others.

You showed me that I should think the best of other people.

You wanted to be a part of my world, and you carved your place in it.

You never treated me like a stupid child.

You were happy to let our relationship evolve at its own pace.

Sometimes you call for no reason, just to hear the sound of my voice.

Your kindness to my friends, even those you didn't really approve of, made me proud to be your child.

You were never too proud to say you were sorry.

"Whenever I did something as a little girl—learn to swim, or act in a school play, for instance—he was fabulous. There would be this certain look in his eyes. It made me feel great."

DIANE KEATON

Our difference in age never seems an issue when we are together— we're friends, and we always will be.

You showed me that there's a difference between showing strength and being stubborn.

You always make me feel good about myself.

We have our own special shorthand that no one else would understand.

You always forgave me, and that taught me to cherish forgiveness.

You were polite and welcoming to my partners— even the really weird ones!

You never told me I had to choose between you and something else.

Even if you were angry when I confessed mistakes, I knew that you would help me correct them.

You made me believe that you shared my insecurities and that everything I felt was entirely normal.

The sun wasn't allowed to set on any of our disagreements.

You never hesitated to walk the path beside me, even when it was slippery.

You've got no idea how often I begin a sentence with the phrase, "My dad says."

You were always kind to my friends, and I was proud to have them meet you.

You made sure I understood how brave it can be to apologize.

You never made me feel that if I failed, I'd disappoint you.

"I am many things besides, but I am Daddy's girl and so I will remain—all the way to the old folks' home."

PAULA WEIDEGER

You didn't hold rewards or punishments over my head to make me behave.

You gave me the freedom in which our friendship could grow.

I always want to know what you think of people, because your instincts are right on target.

You talked me through things with patience and intelligence.

When I irritate you, you take a deep breath and count to ten rather than snap.

Your warm encouragement has made you the best friend I've ever had.

You never forgot to call when you were away on business.

You told me to make sure I valued my real friends.

The greatest gift you ever gave me was your friendship.

6

Living Together

You helped with my homework but you wouldn't do it for me, no matter how much I pleaded.

"There comes a time when you have to face the fact that Dad has forgotten how to do algebra."
CHARLOTTE GRAY

You taught me time management, but let it fly out the window when we were having fun.

I liked looking at the moon and the stars with you.

You made me believe I was a good person inside, despite my bad moods.

Your old slippers still remind me of the times we sat down together and just talked.

Your cheerful grin in the morning
was the perfect start to my day.

"Your father knows what you need before you ask him."

MATTHEW 6:8

You ran my bath at just
the right temperature.

You made my toast just the way I liked it.

You were the hub of our home, the center we revolved around.

You were the best at putting bandages on scraped knees.

You had such an air of competence, I never realized when you didn't know what you were doing.

You almost always found time to read me a bedtime story.

You made sure I was calm and content before I fell asleep.

You hated my fussy eating, and you never gave up trying to expand my tastes.

"If the new American father feels bewildered and even defeated, let him take comfort from the fact that whatever he does in any fathering situation has a 50 percent chance of being right."

BILL COSBY

You allowed me to change my mind over and over and over again.

You have a disapproving look that I recognize instantly, but you use it sparingly.

Sometimes I would be grumpy when I didn't get my own way, but deep down I was glad you gave me clear boundaries.

The pictures I have of just the two of us show me a warm bond that I never really appreciated at the time.

You never had a problem with multitasking—you were always happy to answer all my questions while trying to tend the garden, build a model, or wash the dishes.

You always found the places where I hadn't washed properly.

You never felt the need to control me, and you allowed me to find peace in being myself.

I was never scared to show you a school report card, because I knew you would accentuate the positives rather than dwell on negatives.

You knew me better than I knew myself.

Thank you, Dad, for forcing me to brush my teeth!

You kept me calm around exam times.

You never gave up when I was slow to master the art of tying my shoelaces.

You listened with fascination to everything my teachers had to say about me.

You save leftovers, string, and wrapping paper, but as far as I know, you never use them.

You're good at dealing with creepy-crawlies.

In restaurants, you always want to taste everyone else's food.

I liked to do chores side by side with you.

You always complimented the dishes I cooked, even when they resembled mud pies!

I used to love your little domestic idiosyncracies, and now I realize that I have adopted some of them myself.

I liked to watch you frowning as you tried to fix some toy of mine.

You understood that occasionally eating enough cotton candy to make yourself sick is not the end of the world.

The best sound of childhood
was your key in the door.

You were generous
with your time as
well as your money.

You have some very bizarre and utterly useless skills.

You'd do anything to make me happy, but you never let me wrap you around my little finger.

Our time together was always the highlight of my day.

You made me realize that surviving the bad times will make the good times even better.

You protected my eyes from the shampoo when you washed my hair.

In retrospect, I realize you saw through every fib I ever told, but you didn't always make an issue of it.

You respected my privacy and didn't poke through my personal belongings.

You say you were never patient before you became a father.

You always had some spare change to give me.

You always seem to enjoy my company.

I loved the moments when you set aside your papers and gave me your time.

You always had great ideas for treats when I needed cheering up.

When I couldn't get to sleep at night, you lay quietly beside me to calm me down.

I remember how much you delighted in my enjoyment of new experiences.

You understood that a hug and a sip of water dispelled even the worst nightmares.

"A king, realizing his incompetence, can either delegate or abdicate his duties. A father can do neither. If only sons could see the paradox, they would understand the dilemma."

MARLENE DIETRICH

I know your taste in food, and I like buying your favorites for you.

When you dressed up, you made me want to look as nice as you did.

When your favorite songs come on the radio, I smile and think of you.

You remember and quote my funny toddler sayings.

"A father is a guy who has snapshots in his wallet where his money used to be."
ANONYMOUS

You still manage to surprise me all the time.

You taught me to value the happy accidents in life.

You let your cup of coffee grow cold time after time because I was more important.

I used to sit in your chair until you came home because it held your shape and gave me a special link to you.

You obeyed the "keep out" sign on my door.

You were happy to get down and play on the floor with me.

You'd spend hours constructing complex toys from kits for me.

You never tried to bribe me to succeed or to do what you wanted.

You never made me feel that I had to be sneaky to get my own way.

On my birthday, you always talk about the day I was born.

You love to reminisce about all the fun we've had.

You understood that at times I needed to be alone.

You're not averse to between-meals snacks, and you didn't try to stop me from having them.

I loved the way my homemade cards and gifts pleased you the most (or at least you pretended they did).

You were always full of admiration for my efforts.

You're good at opening jars that have very tight lids.

You get irritable when your cooking efforts fail.

I used to believe you could fix anything, but it didn't shake my faith in you to discover that there are exceptions.

You taught me the meaning of courtesy by giving it to me.

You always made me feel that my needs came first.

I used to disregard your advice, but I always listened to it first.

You didn't get cross when I woke up early on birthdays.

You know how to head
off confrontation.

*I remember I was very proud when I
learned how to make you a cup of coffee.*

Whether we stayed at home or
went on a trip, you always made
summer vacations interesting.

You made me value being practical and capable.

Sometimes you tried to pretend to like my music, which was a bit embarrassing.

You never had a problem with the physical side of parenting, like changing diapers and wiping runny noses.

You always meant it when you said, "no," but you took the time to explain why.

You filled the house with interesting objects, so there was always something to pick up and contemplate in idle moments.

You were never afraid to go into the basement on your own in the dark.

There are so many family photos you're not in, because you were the one taking them.

You never made a fuss about spills, stains, or dirty clothes.

I wouldn't say that I can wind you around my little finger, but I can usually find a way to get what I want.

"'Father' is rather vulgar, my dear. The word 'Papa,' besides, gives a very pretty form to the lips."
CHARLES DICKENS

You always remember exactly how I like my coffee.

I know you would give me the last chocolate in the box.

You always let me have the seat with the best view.

I love the smell of your old sweaters.

You could untie my shoelaces when I had tugged so hard the knot was tiny.

You were good at answering questions like "why is the sky blue?" and "why do bees sting?"

A sunny morning always filled you with good humor and now it does the same for me.

You enjoy the passing of the seasons and the changes in the weather.

You've shown me the comfort of an evening spent in front of the fire with a good book.

You made sure I understood that everyone in a family has a responsibility to it.

I catch myself using some of your favorite phrases and sayings.

"Dad is proud of the buildings he's put up over the years. To me, none of these can match the little things he made just for me with his two hands."

SUZANNE CHAZIN

You knew the power of a reward.

Our evening chats help to put the day in perspective.

You were always my best alarm clock.

A meal out together was always a special treat, and it still is today.

You did your best to buy me the material things I wanted, even when you thought they were a waste of money.

Maybe all dads steal french fries from their kids' plates, but I think you invented some of the most ingenious tactics.

You do your best to avoid arguments and fights.

"You know, fathers just have a way of putting everything together."
ERIKA COSBY

You never made me feel useless because I was just starting out.

Your idea of breakfast is the same as mine: anything goes!

You were a "new man" long before the media invented such a term.

You've always been good at surprises!

Sometimes you looked the other way when you had every right to be angry.

You always told me I was good-looking, although there is no doubt that I was an ugly duckling.

You never mind comfortable silences when we are together; our closeness speaks more than words.

You understood that life is sweeter with the occasional treat.

I felt very important when you let me stay up late to watch a TV program with you.

Where there was a problem, you found a solution.

You are not a person who ever admits defeat.

"A father is a banker provided by nature."
FRENCH PROVERB

You tell a good story!

You've mastered the art of puttering, while claiming that you are busy with some dreadfully important business.

You make sure that treats are on the menu when you're in charge.

You always understood the restorative powers of a chocolate biscuit.

Half asleep, I felt you kiss me goodnight before I snuggled back into my dreams.

At one time our home was my whole world; then, as I grew up, it became the center of my world.

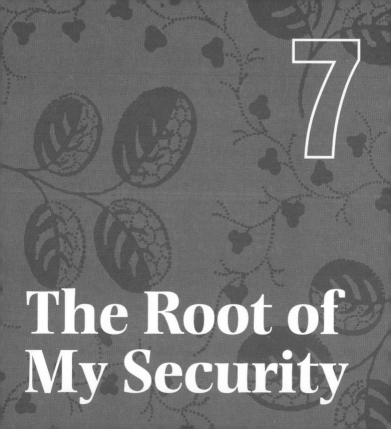

7

The Root of
My Security

You're the one who was always able to make the nightmares go away.

When we went out in the cold, you fussed over my gloves and jacket and hat.

The world wouldn't feel like such a safe place without you in it.

You took your role as a father seriously, but with tenderness.

When I hear dramatic news on the TV or radio, I always call to see if you've heard it, too.

Even when we're far apart, I find comfort knowing that you're thinking about me.

You're my personal doctor, teacher, therapist, and social worker all rolled into one.

I know that no matter how much time passes or how far I travel, there's always a place for me at home.

When I face a problem I still think to myself, "What would Dad do?"

You've never tried to make me suffer the hardships and problems that you had in life.

"I just owe almost everything to my father."
MARGARET THATCHER

You don't make promises that you can't keep.

On your shoulders, anchored by your steady grip, I could look out at the world.

You let me venture out and find my own way, but you placed a hand on my shoulder when I needed reassurance.

You showed me that in the face of life's uncertainties, I could always rely on you.

When I was ill, your care and concern were almost overwhelming.

You knew your responsibilities didn't end when I left home; that instead, a whole new set had begun.

Sometimes I've taken the right path just because I couldn't bear to disappoint you.

You looked out for me, but you also let me learn some hard lessons for myself.

When I thought of running away from home, I always knew I could come back.

After a day of falls, bumps, and mishaps, you gave me the familiar comfort of your arms and made me feel safe again.

When you went to work, I knew it was to take care of us.

"How sweet it is to sit 'neath a fond father's smile."

JOHN HOWARD PAYNE

Now that I'm an adult, I'm awed by the job you did at being a good father.

You'd always swoop down to rescue me if I was threatened in any way.

You let me know that you were always there at the end of the phone.

You'd jump in your car at a moment's notice if you thought I needed you.

You make sure I always know
where I can find you.

You never made me
feel I owed you anything
for bringing me up.

I never worried that you might
resent my success in life.

I always knew you would be coming home.

You never missed an occasion that was important to me.

Whenever I was involved in a dispute, you would listen to both sides of the story.

Even when I did things that made you very unhappy, you kept your composure.

You made sure you said, "Good job!" when you saw I'd tried hard.

The word "home" just makes me feel good.

I wasn't afraid of the dark
when I knew you were there.

You didn't pretend that
life is always a breeze.

*You tried to show me how good
things can come from bad.*

Your secret was always to figure out how to turn failure into success.

You've seen me at my worst and you haven't batted an eyelid.

You always kept your word, and you taught me to keep mine.

I remember being snuggled beneath your coat, safe from the elements and the outside world.

Dozing against you as night fell is one of my coziest memories.

You made me realize that I was worth something.

You shrunk to my size when we played, and expanded to great heights when I needed shelter and protection.

You made sure I never resented not being the center of attention.

When I've been really low and despondent, you've always helped to encourage me.

"My dear father! When I remember him, it is always with his arms open wide to love and comfort me."
ISOBEL FIELD

I used to fit perfectly on your lap,
with my head on your shoulder.

*You help me to
center myself.*

You always seem to have
a handkerchief.

When I'm in a panic, you
provide an oasis of calm.

You never stopped me from going where my friends were going, but you always made sure that I got home safely afterward.

You have never betrayed my trust.

You made sure I had the confidence to stand up and be heard.

When I had a bad day and needed to hide away, you didn't force me to be sociable.

You showed me that no trouble is so bad that it can't be overcome.

When I faced tough times, I knew you were right behind me.

You never told me I wasn't up to the job.

I owe you so much, but you never make me feel it.

You always showed me that sharing is more fun in the long run.

I've never regretted being a part of your family.

"And how my father loved
and watched us,
and guarded our happiness."
EDGAR LEE MASTERS

You taught me that I could rely on myself.

I always knew that if I had a problem,
you would make it your priority.

You're the anchor that stops me from getting swept away and shipwrecked.

I can't imagine anything that would make you fall apart.

You always tempered punishment with tenderness.

I believed you were always right, and even though we all make mistakes, you usually were.

I've never been afraid to tell you the truth.

Because you treated me as a responsible person, I always took responsibility.

When I think of home, it makes me feel warm inside.

Because of you, I don't fear change.

Your hugs are one of the nicest feelings I know.

I've never been afraid that you might let me down.

You've never brushed my feelings aside.

I knew that if I wanted to know the truth, you would tell me.

You always explained the reasons behind what you did.

You always did your best to make sure I grew up healthy and strong.

You made me confident that there was a happy ending waiting for me.

You've made me treasure close relationships, not fear them.

Home has never been a particular house, but wherever you are.

You gave me a home that was full of warmth, light, and laughter.

You did all you could to make my world a safer place.

You held my hand when I was frightened, and you made me feel protected.

When I hurt myself, you were there to comfort and heal me.

When my storms of tears were over, you were there to mop me up.

You never felt threatened by my growing up.

You wiped my tears, bandaged my wounds, and made me realize that I could try again.

You didn't want to lock me away from the world.

You taught me to fight my own battles, but you were always there in the background.

"[He] adopted a role called Being a Father so that his child would have something mythical and infinitely important: a Protector, who would keep a lid on all the chaotic and catastrophic possibilities of life."

TOM WOLFE

You've got a great sense of direction, and you stop me from getting lost.

It's not just my problems you help me with; I ask your advice on behalf of my friends, too.

When you come to my house, you always find something to fix.

I don't think I've ever seen you scared of anything.

You always find a logical explanation for spooky noises in the night.

Even now, you still remind me to dress warmly if it's chilly out.

When I have a cold, you call to check on me.

You were there, my hero, for every little thing I needed.

You let me climb as high as I could, even when your knuckles were white with fear.

I know you will always catch me if I fall.

I never felt quite complete until I knew you were home.

I loved the way you tucked me in at night.

You helped me to rely on my instincts and trust my feelings.

Like a caveman, you feel a primeval responsibility to make sure I'm warm, safe, and well fed—even now that I've left home!

You've shown me that there's a place for me in the world.

You tell me not to worry about things that might never happen.

You smooth my anxieties and relieve my cares.

I could never have taken the risks I've taken in my life if I didn't know I had you there as a safety net.

You always stuck by me, even when you doubted my motives.

My greatest need was for your protection, and you never let me down.

You always forgive me, even when I don't really deserve it.

"Safe, for a child, is his father's hand, holding him tight."
MARION C. GARRETTY

You made me believe you could do anything—and through that, I believed I could, too.

You never judge me too harshly.

When you threw me high in the air, I never doubted for a second that you would catch me.

Sometimes you still try to keep sad things from me because you don't want to cloud my happy world.

You never acted as though you were too busy to care for me.

It made me feel important when you took my fears and concerns seriously.

You never pretended I didn't have any faults.

You never told me to go away or to "grow up."

I liked it when it rained and we were all safe inside.

I need your protection less now than I used to, but I still need to know it's there.

"My father died many years ago, and yet when something special happens to me, I talk to him secretly, not really knowing whether he hears, but it makes me feel better to half believe it."

NATASHA JOSEFOWITZ

The only time I saw you really angry was when you believed that I had been harmed.

You never hold a grudge; you know that disagreements are just short-term problems to be overcome.

Your anxiety about my safety was well hidden, but I saw a glimpse of it from time to time, and it made me feel like the most important child on Earth.

Whatever life throws at you, I know you will be capable of handling it.

You made sure that, while the adult world was strange, it didn't seem frightening.

I never worried that you would turn me away. Not ever.

A roaring fire and a comforting hug from you always kept the trials of the outside world at bay.

After a trip you always want me to phone to let you know I've made it home safely.

You never made me think that you couldn't handle the job of being a parent, or made me wait for something until Mom got home.

You tucked me in so that I felt safe and protected from anything the darkness might hold.

If I lost all my money, I know you would support me.

On your list of priorities, you make me feel that I come first.

"I cannot think of any need in childhood as strong as the need for a father's protection."
SIGMUND FREUD

You always defended me, even when you were not absolutely sure that I was right.

You were always the dispenser of justice, and even when I disagreed with your methods, I knew you were always fair.

When I was sick you went to the drugstore to get my medicine.

You took pleasure in my dependence upon you, and you never made me feel like a burden.

"The thing to remember about fathers is, they're men. A girl has to keep it in mind: They are dragon-seekers, bent on improbable rescues."

PHYLLIS MCGINLEY

The weight of responsibility you must have felt never showed.

In most situations, you seemed to possess unlimited reserves of patience.

You always had time to sit down and work through a problem with me.

You could always explain away threatening shadows on the walls.

"A dad is a man haunted by death, fears, anxieties. But who seems to his children the haven from all harm."

CLARA ORTEGA

You showed me how to see the light at the end of the tunnel.

Even as an adult, there's a part of me that still believes you will always somehow be able to make everything all right.

You often took the blame for my mistakes yourself.

No matter how difficult things were for you, you never burdened me with your problems.

Your genuine sympathy and understanding helped me survive my first heartbreak.

Even now, when I am sad or upset, my thoughts turn to you.

You nag me about insurance and savings because you want me to have financial security.

"All about him was safe."
NAOMI MITCHISON

You chased away the monsters under my bed.

I feel so lucky when I remember how happy my childhood was.

Your Inspiration

You always told me I could do anything and go anywhere, and that broadened my horizons.

No matter what you're doing, you never do less than your best.

You've always had complete faith in me, even when I've felt low and useless.

You were always capable of dreaming the biggest dreams.

You've always inspired me with your enthusiasm for everything life has to offer.

You're always excited about the things I achieve in life, but my failures don't bother you.

You made me realize that there is no substitute for a happy childhood and a loving family.

You gave me the foundation I needed for a well-balanced life.

You have a newspaper clipping or story to match every one of my budding interests.

When people compliment me, I always know I owe it to you.

"My mother and father are the only people on the whole planet for whom I will never begrudge a thing. Should I achieve great things, it is the work of their hands."

ANTON CHEKHOV

You taught me that as long as I am happy with myself, I will lead a satisfied life.

You never let anyone walk all over you—except me, sometimes.

My view of the world has been so enriched by what you've shown me.

You used your hands, your mind, and your heart to show me the world.

You've never let go of your dreams for yourself or for me.

It's because of you that I've been able to form healthy relationships in my life.

You opened my eyes to what other countries could offer me.

You worked hard and set a great example for me, then didn't mind when I went my own way.

"How true Daddy's words were when he said: 'All children must look after their own upbringing.'"

ANNE FRANK

You made sure I was able to hold on to the magic of childhood for as long as possible.

You opened the doors of my imagination.

You've never lost your interest in life and everything around you.

You never tried to change just to please others.

"My father instilled in me that if you don't see things happening the way you want them to, you get out there and make them happen."

SUSAN POWTER

No parent is ever perfect, but I know you did your best, and I hope I am a credit to you.

Your sense of **justice** **defined** mine.

Your pride in me made me believe in myself.

Your belief in me was always enough to get me through periods of self-doubt.

You took **pride** in turning your hand to **anything** at all.

You made me realize that one person can definitely make a difference in the world.

Because of you, I have the strength to defend the things I believe in.

Sometimes I wonder how you got to be so wise!

"If the relationship of father to son could really be reduced to biology, the whole earth would blaze with the glory of fathers and sons."
JAMES BALDWIN

You always rose to the challenge of being held in such high esteem by me.

Your inquisitive mind made me want to ask questions, too.

You made me think that there were no limits to what I could achieve.

You helped me to treasure beautiful things.

You opened my eyes to so much the world has to offer.

You were always eager to pass on your enthusiasm for your favorite things.

"When I was a kid, my father told me every day, 'You're the most wonderful boy in the world, and you can do anything you want to.' "

JAN HUTCHINS

You showed me that "expensive" doesn't necessarily mean "good."

You've inspired me to take my role as a member of society seriously.

You showed me that the smartest people are the ones who know how much they still have to learn.

Your enthusiasm for everything the world has to offer has made me want to do my bit to protect it.

I've never forgotten the way you hate cruelty.

You're **always ready** to rush to the side of the **underdog**.

You've never become jaded or blasé about life.

"Let my father's honours live in me."
WILLIAM SHAKESPEARE

You showed me how to make the best of any situation.

You taught me that anger and distress will always pass.

You've made me value the company of my elders.

You were frank about the importance of using my opportunities.

I know that your core values will never change.

Nothing seems to faze you, and I'd like to imitate that.

If I amount to anything, it's due to you.

You would never make fun of my ambitions or tell me they're unrealistic.

You found miracles in even the most tedious days.

"One man with courage makes a majority."

ANDREW JACKSON

You taught me that I'm worthy of the good things in life.

Because of you, I value the gift of learning.

You made me see the wonder and ingenuity of an anthill.

You brought so much color into my world.

You often think of an angle I've overlooked.

"My father gave me the greatest gift anyone could give another person; he believed in me."
JIM VALVANO

Your optimism has helped me through the dark times.

You made me interested in the things you are passionate about.

You were the making of me—you were so true to me and so sure of me.

I saw myself in you, and I liked what I saw.

You've always embraced the new, and shown me how to as well.

If people tell me I'm a good person, I know the credit is yours.

You have a project or dream that you're excited about.

You're always ready to work to solve things.

You're genuinely interested in my career, and you regularly ask about it.

You've made me realize that life never stands still.

You trusted me to go places alone, and that gave me courage.

Like you, I try not to rush things before I've thought them through.

You made me realize that life will always have pitfalls, and that they are to be overcome, not feared.

You showed me how to enjoy the beauty in the world.

"*My father did enough in his lifetime to answer for both of us.*"
WOODROW WILSON

You've made me feel that everything is within my reach.

I couldn't ask for a more inspiring mentor.

I hope I can live as rich and rewarding a life as you.

You taught me to join in with the singing, even if I didn't know the words.

Your example taught me
not to let bad feelings and
resentment fester.

You showed me that
I need to care for our
environment and do
what I can to protect it.

I'm moved by your gentleness with the weak and helpless.

I love the way you're still building castles in the air.

You've taught me to be a dreamer with my feet on the ground.

You help me see that love and relationships are the most valuable things of all.

Your happiness with your life made everyone around you happy, too.

"*The words that a father speaks to his children in the privacy of home are not heard by the world, but, as in whispering galleries, they are clearly heard at the end, and by posterity.*"

JEAN PAUL RICHTER

You make me **feel** that **fatherhood** is your proudest **achievement.**

I cherish every moment we have together, because life is unpredictable.

Who else would treasure all the paintings I brought home from school as if they were Picassos?

You slowed me down so that I could see the world around me.

My dreams became yours, and you inspired me to chase them with you.

You let me choose my own path, and you never made me believe I'd taken the wrong one.

You showed me that simple things, such as walking the dog, made a man a king in his own world.

You sometimes have to wipe away a tear when you hear beautiful music.

Your fearlessness helped me to overcome my own fears.

"When a child, my dreams rode on your wishes, I was your son, high on your horse."

STEPHEN SPENDER

You're my touchstone for all that is wise and good and true in the world.

You taught me that we're all just passing through, and to value every second we get.

You wanted me to be a credit to you,
but never at my own expense.

You always helped me see magic in the little things.

You understood the meaning of self-esteem long before the concept became fashionable.

We've gone through periods of being close, and then times when we're not so close, but there is still a look in your eye that can make me feel great.

Although I dismissed so many of them at the time, your words often come back to comfort me.

Your uncritical style of love left me free to bestow love.

You made me see the riches that the world has, both natural and man-made.

You are usually happy with the way things are, and you don't spend a lot of effort trying to force change.

You showed me how to keep the door open to opportunity.

You taught me to aim for the moon if I believed in something.

You didn't laugh at my crazy fantasies of what I wanted to do with my life.

I don't think you'll ever stop wanting to broaden your horizons.

"**Directly after God in heaven comes Papa.**"

WOLFGANG AMADEUS MOZART

I love hearing your opinions about anything at all.

Because of you, the word "father" is full of warmth for me.

The boyish delight that eclipses your face sometimes lets me glimpse the child you once were, and makes me love you even more.

You convinced me that I'm special.

Because of you, I have a center to my world.

"Dad" is such a small word, when you think of all the big emotions that go with it.

It's not much to say, but—thank you.